BOOK 1

HARMONY LESSONS

By JOHN W. SCHAUM

Highlights of the Schaum Harmony Lessons

Harmony has been called the "grammar of music." You can study English grammar from grade school through college and find that you still have much to learn. It is the same with music; harmony is a subject from which you can always learn something new.

The Schaum *Harmony Lessons** is a series of two books. The purpose is to present basic fundamentals to the music student without going into professional technicalities. However, the aspects of harmony presented in these books form a solid foundation, which is essential for those aspiring to a musical career.

These books are intended for use by a piano teacher as part of a regular lesson. They can also be used by instrumental and vocal teachers who want their students to know some of the elements of harmony but who do not have the time to teach it as a separate subject.

Each lesson has a concise explanation and directions that are easy to understand. Minimal help is needed from the teacher at the lesson. The assignments can be done by the student at home, thereby saving precious lesson time.

The lessons are in workbook form. Space is provided for all written assignments in the book, eliminating the need for extra music manuscript paper. There is a quiz at the end of each book to determine how well the subject matter has been retained.

Transposition has been treated both as melody and harmony. Toward the end of Book 2, harmony is treated as an accompaniment rather than as four-part harmony.

*The student should have completed the Schaum *Note Speller*, Book 2 (EL00221A), and Schaum *Theory Lessons*, Book 3 (EL00414A), as prerequisites.

Editor: Wesley Schaum
Project Manager: Gail Lew
Art Design: Lisa Mane and Carmen Fortunato

Contents Book One

Contents Book Two

Lesson 1. Finding the Tonic

Name_____ Date_____ Grade_____

The *first note* of a scale is called the **tonic.** It is considered the most important note of a scale. To find the tonic in sharp keys, GO UP ONE HALF STEP from the LAST SHARP (the sharp in the key signature that is farthest from the clef sign). For example, if the key signature has two sharps, the last sharp is C♯. Going up one half step from C♯ is D. Therefore, D is the tonic.

DIRECTIONS: Write the key name and draw a whole note to indicate the tonic in each of the following examples. The sample is correctly marked.

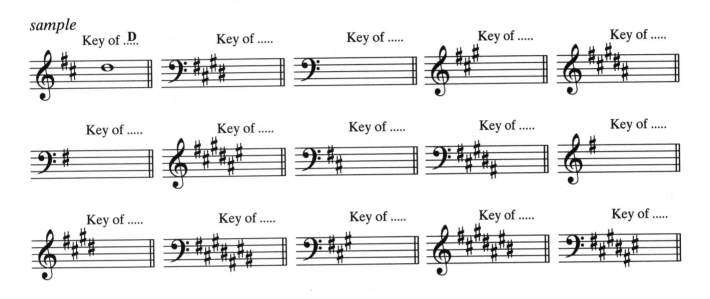

In flat keys, the tonic has the SAME NAME as the SECOND LAST FLAT of the key signature. For example, if the key signature has three flats, the second last flat is E♭. Therefore, the tonic is E♭. Exception to the rule: if the key signature has only one flat (B♭), the tonic is F.

DIRECTIONS: Write the key name and draw a whole note to indicate the tonic in each of the following examples. The sample is correctly marked.

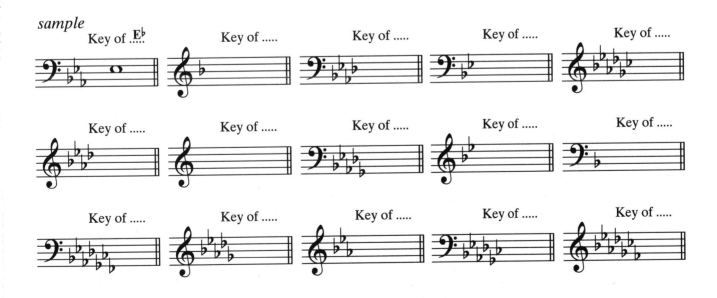

KEYBOARD ASSIGNMENT: Play all of the above tonic notes on the piano.

Lesson 2. Major Scale Review (Sharp Keys)

Name _____ Date _____ Grade_____

> The major scale can be divided into two tetrachords *one whole step apart*. A **tetrachord** is a series of four notes with the following intervals between them:
>
> **1**   (whole step)   **2**   (whole step)   **3**   (half step)   **4**
>
> The notes in each staff below form a different major scale. The first staff has the C major scale (no sharps in the key signature). The second staff has the G major scale (1 sharp in the key signature). The major scale in each staff that follows adds one more sharp to its key signature (2 sharps, 3 sharps, 4 sharps, etc.).
>
> Notice that the notes (G-A-B-C) of the **second** tetrachord of the C major scale are the *same* as the notes (G-A-B-C) of the **first** tetrachord of the G major scale on the staff below. This same tetrachord relationship continues between all of the staffs that follow. For example, the **second** tetrachord of the G major scale is the same as the **first** tetrachord of the D major scale. This is shown in the samples printed below.

DIRECTIONS: Draw whole notes for the tetrachords on the staffs below. Use the intervals: W = Whole step, H = Half step. Remember, there is also a whole step *between* the two tetrachords. Use accidental sharps as needed for the tetrachord notes; do not use key signatures. Then draw the sharps for each key signature in the column at the right.

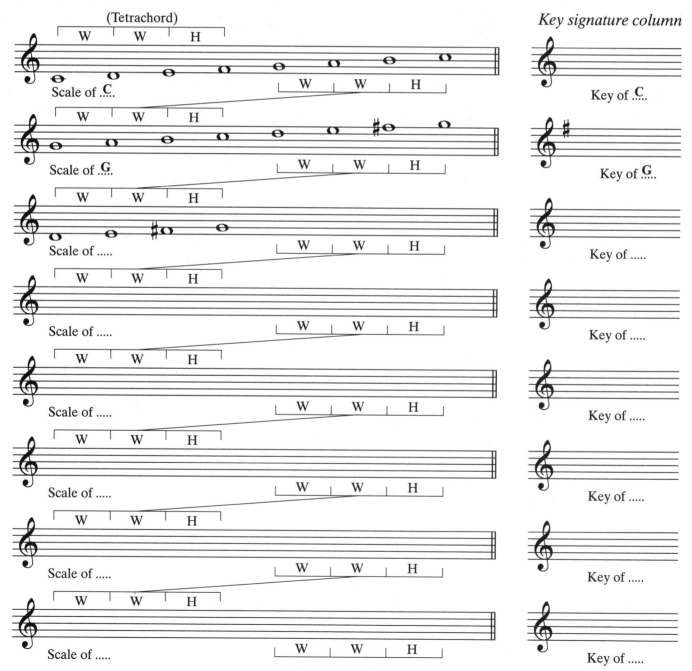

Lesson 3. Major Scale Review (Flat Keys)

Name_____ Date _____ Grade_____

The notes in each staff below form a different major scale. The first staff has the C major scale (no flats in the key signature). The second staff has the F major scale (1 flat in the key signature). The major scale in each staff that follows adds one more flat to its key signature (2 flats, 3 flats, 4 flats, etc.).

Notice that the notes (C-D-E-F) of the **first** tetrachord of the C major scale are the same as the notes (C-D-E-F) of the **second** tetrachord of the F major scale on the staff below. This same tetrachord relationship continues between all of the staffs that follow. For example, the **first** tetrachord of the F major scale is the same as the **second** tetrachord of the B♭ major scale. This is shown in the samples printed below.

DIRECTIONS: Draw whole notes for the tetrachords on the staffs below. Use the intervals: W = Whole step, H = Half step. Remember, there is also a whole step *between* the two tetrachords. Use accidental flats as needed for the tetrachord notes; do not use key signatures. Then draw the flats for each key signature in the column at the right.

Lesson 4. Sequence of Sharp Key Signatures

Name_____ Date _____ Grade_____

The key names of major scales with *sharps* follow part of a sequence called the **circle of 5ths** (see Lesson 8). When one sharp is added to the key signature, the scale name changes by the interval of a 5th. For example, notice that the 5th scale note of C major is **G**. The key signature of 1 sharp indicates the key of **G** major.

key signature has no sharps:	key of C major	5th scale note = G
key signature has 1 sharp:	key of G major	5th scale note = D
key signature has 2 sharps:	key of D major	5th scale note = A

Samples of this sequence of 5ths are shown in the *Name of Key* column in the diagram below.

The sharps in a key signature always follow the same sequence. For example, F♯ is always the first sharp, C♯ is always the second sharp, G♯ is always the third sharp, etc. This is shown in the samples printed in the diagram below.

DIRECTIONS: In the *Name of Key* column of the following diagram, write the names of all the sharp keys, following the circle of 5ths, as described above. In the remaining boxes, write the names of the sharps in each key signature.

Number of Sharps	Name of Key	1st Sharp	2nd Sharp	3rd Sharp	4th Sharp	5th Sharp	6th Sharp	7th Sharp
Zero Sharps	C							
One Sharp	G	F♯						
Two Sharps	D	F♯	C♯					
Three Sharps								
Four Sharps								
Five Sharps								
Six Sharps								
Seven Sharps								

DIRECTIONS: Each of the following key signatures has one sharp that is wrong. Cross out the incorrect sharp in each signature. Watch for changes of clef. The sample is correctly marked.

sample

KEYBOARD ASSIGNMENT: Play the seven sharps on the piano in key signature order.

Lesson 5. Sequence of Flat Key Signatures

Name_____ Date _____ Grade_____

> The key names of major scales with *flats* follow part of a sequence called the **circle of 4ths** (see Lesson 9). When one flat is added to the key signature, the scale name changes by the interval of a 4th. For example, notice that the 4th scale note of C major is F. The key signature of 1 flat indicates the key of **F** major.
>
> | key signature has no flats: | key of C major | 4th scale note = F |
> | key signature has 1 flat: | key of F major | 4th scale note = B♭ |
> | key signature has 2 flats: | key of B♭ major | 4th scale note = E♭ |
>
> Samples of this sequence of 4ths are shown in the *Name of Key* column in the diagram below.
>
> The flats in a key signature always follow the same sequence. For example, B♭ is always the first flat, E♭ is always the second flat, A♭ is always the third flat, etc. This is shown in the samples printed in the diagram below.

DIRECTIONS: In the *Name of Key* column of the following diagram, write the names of all the flat keys, following the circle of 4ths, as described above. In the remaining boxes, write the names of the flats in each key signature.

Number of Flats	Name of Key	1st Flat	2nd Flat	3rd Flat	4th Flat	5th Flat	6th Flat	7th Flat
Zero Flats	C							
One Flat	F	B♭						
Two Flats	B♭	B♭	E♭					
Three Flats								
Four Flats								
Five Flats								
Six Flats								
Seven Flats								

DIRECTIONS: Each of the following key signatures has one flat that is wrong. Cross out the incorrect flat in each signature. Watch for changes of clef. The sample is correctly marked.

sample

KEYBOARD ASSIGNMENT: Play the seven flats on the piano in key signature order.

Lesson 6. Comparison of Key Signatures

Name _____ Date _____ Grade _____

DIRECTIONS: Fill in the boxes below, listing the order of sharps and flats as indicated. The starting box is filled in as a sample. Fill in the remaining boxes.

SHARPS IN KEY SIGNATURE ORDER						
1st	2nd	3rd	4th	5th	6th	7th
F♯						

FLATS IN KEY SIGNATURE ORDER						
1st	2nd	3rd	4th	5th	6th	7th
B♭						

Now write them in reverse order. Notice that flats are put first.

FLATS IN REVERSE ORDER						
7th	6th	5th	4th	3rd	2nd	1st
F♭						

SHARPS IN REVERSE ORDER						
7th	6th	5th	4th	3rd	2nd	1st
B♯						

Notice the following patterns in the sequence of key signature letter names:

Flats in *reverse* order = Sharps in *regular* order.

Sharps in *reverse* order = Flats in *regular* order.

This will help you to remember the order of sharps and flats in key signatures.

THE SCALES OF C, C♯ AND C♭

DIRECTIONS: On the staffs below, write the notes for the scales of C, C♯ and C♭. Notice that the notes of the C scales are either *all* natural, *all* sharp or *all* flat.

C major (all naturals)

1   2   3   4   5   6   7   8

C♯ major (all sharps)
(insert signature)

1   2   3   4   5   6   7   8

C♭ major (all flats)
(insert signature)

1   2   3   4   5   6   7   8

KEYBOARD ASSIGNMENT: Play the major scales of C, C♯ and C♭.

Lesson 7. Enharmonic Keys

Name _____ Date _____ Grade _____

> **Enharmonic** keys sound the same, but are *spelled differently*. For example, the key of Db major sounds the same as the key of C# major. Db major is easier to read because there are 5 flats in the key signature, whereas C# major has 7 sharps in the key signature.

DIRECTIONS: On the staffs below, draw the notes of the two enharmonic scales, Db major and C# major.

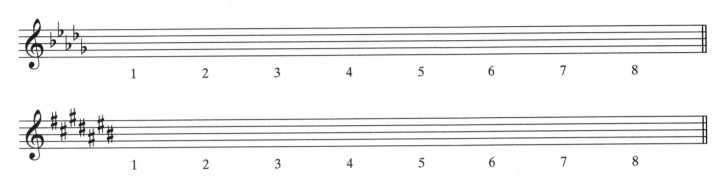

> Gb major and F# major are also *enharmonic*. One key signature has 6 flats, the other has 6 sharps. However, Gb major is used more often in music literature.

DIRECTIONS: On the staffs below, draw the notes of the two enharmonic scales, Gb major and F# major. Watch for the clef sign.

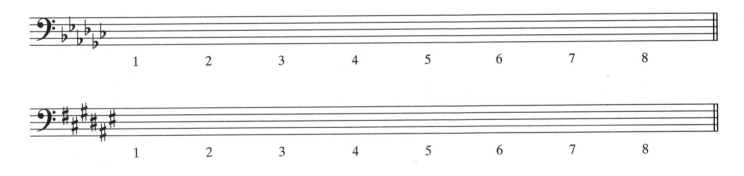

> B major and Cb major are also *enharmonic*. B major is easier to read because there are 5 sharps in the key signature, whereas Cb major has 7 flats in the key signature.

DIRECTIONS: On the staffs below, draw the notes of the two enharmonic scales, B major and Cb major. Watch for the clef sign.

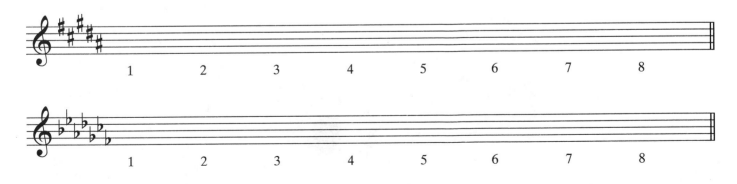

KEYBOARD ASSIGNMENT: Play each pair of enharmonic scales on the piano. Notice that they sound exactly alike.

Lesson 8. Major Key Circle of Fifths

Name _____ Date _____ Grade_____

DIRECTIONS: In each section of the large circular staff, draw the notes of the first **five** scale degrees, going upward. Notice that the **5th** degree of each scale is always the 1st degree of the scale that follows it. Draw the new key signature each time, and write the 1st and 5th letter names in the boxes below the staff.

Compare your answers with the key letter names in the small circle in the center of the diagram. If your answers are correct, they will match with the clockwise letter sequence of the inner circle.

The scales of B major, G♭ major and D♭ major are to be used instead of their *enharmonic* equivalents (C♭ major, F♯ major and C♯ major).

Notice when you finish that you have returned to the same note on which you started.

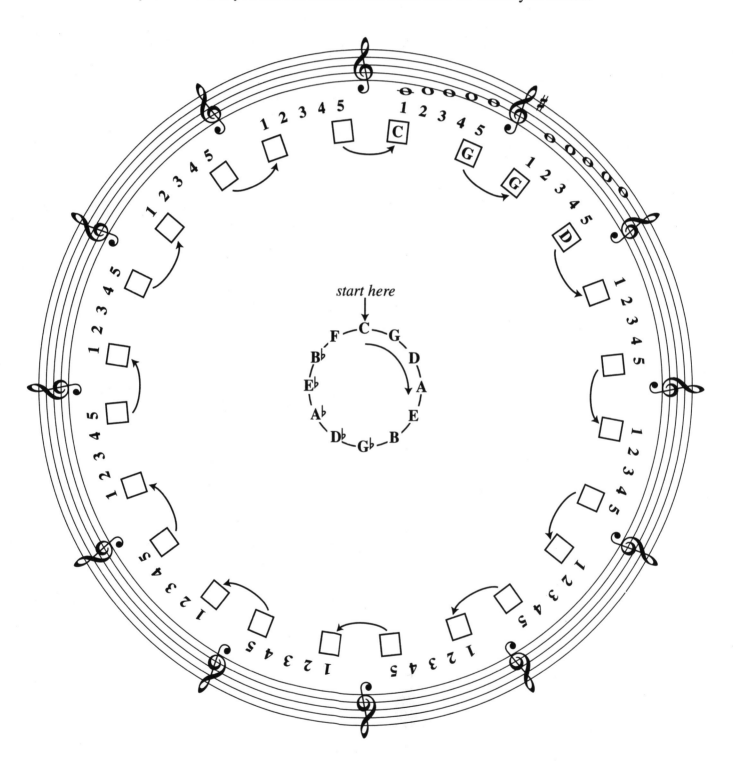

KEYBOARD ASSIGNMENT: Play the major key circle of fifths on the piano, going up five steps each time, just as written.

Lesson 9. Major Key Circle of Fourths

Name _____ Date _____ Grade _____

DIRECTIONS: In each section of the large circular staff, draw the notes of the first **four** scale degrees, going upward. Notice that the **4th** degree of each scale is always the 1st degree of the scale that follows it. Draw the new key signature each time, and write the 1st and 4th letter names in the boxes below the staff.

   Compare your answers with the key letter names in the small circle in the center of the diagram. If your answers are correct, they will match with the clockwise letter sequence of the inner circle.

   The scales of D♭ major, G♭ major and B major are to be used instead of their enharmonic equivalents (C♯ major, F♯ major and C♭ major).

   Notice when you finish that you have returned to the same note on which you started.

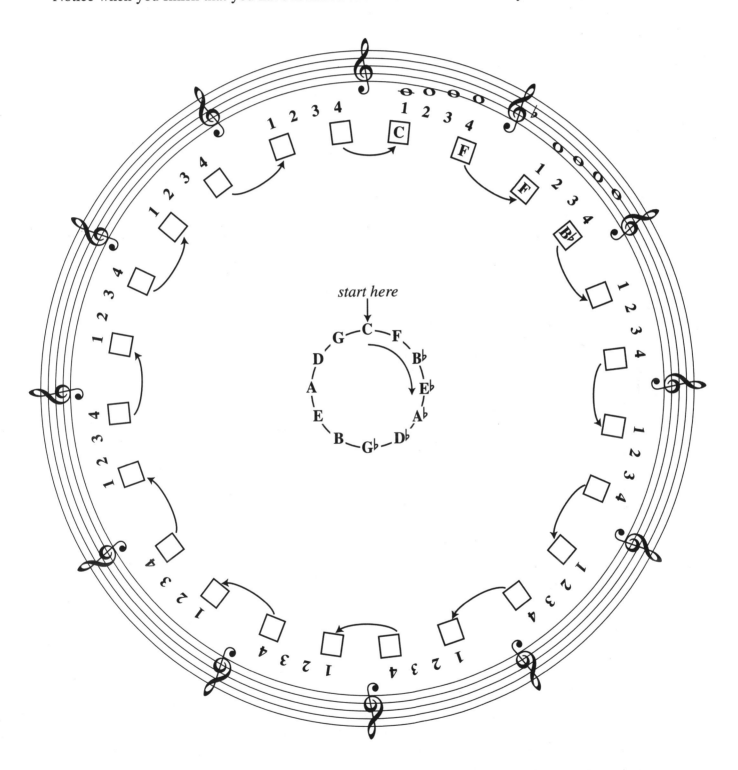

KEYBOARD ASSIGNMENT: Play the major key circle of fourths on the piano, going up four steps each time, just as written. Notice that order of keys in the circle of fourths is the *reverse* of the order in the circle of fifths.

Lesson 10. Scale Number Names

Name _____ Date _____ Grade _____

The notes of a major scale are numbered 1 through 8. These numbers are sometimes called **degrees**.
The 1st scale degree is the same as the *tonic* note (see Lesson 1).

DIRECTIONS: On the staffs below, draw the appropriate scale note above each number. Watch for changes of clef.

sample

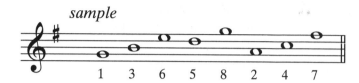

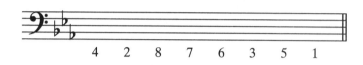

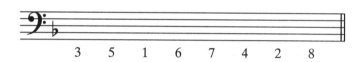

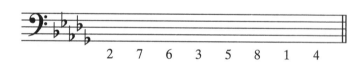

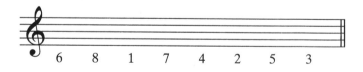

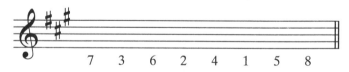

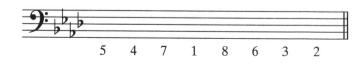

KEYBOARD ASSIGNMENT: Play all the scale notes you have written above.

Lesson 11. Transposing with Scale Degree Numbers

Name _____ Date _____ Grade _____

An excerpt from "Blue Bells of Scotland" is printed here, with scale degree numbers below each note. The measures at the end of each staff have notes and scale degree numbers from other keys. These are to be used as reference when doing the transposing on this page.

DIRECTIONS: Transpose the melody "Blue Bells of Scotland," to the five keys indicated below. Refer to the scale degree numbers at the end of each staff. Watch for different key signatures.

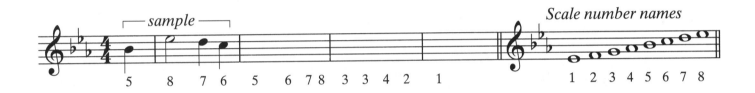

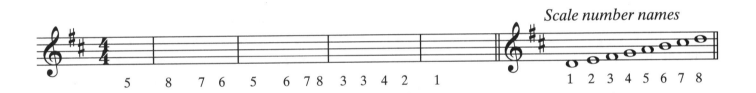

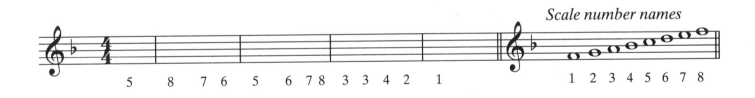

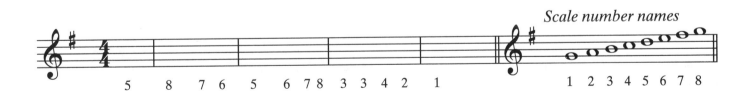

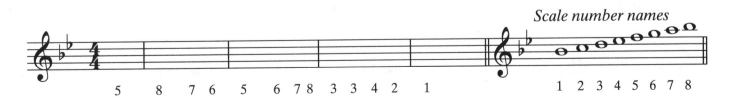

KEYBOARD ASSIGNMENT: Play the excerpt from "Blue Bells of Scotland" in each of the transposed keys.

Lesson 12. Melodic and Harmonic Intervals

Name _____ Date _____ Grade _____

An **interval** is the distance between two notes. Two notes, played *one after the other*, are a **melodic** interval. Two notes played *together* are a **harmonic** interval. This is shown in the following examples:

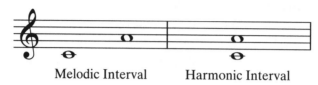

Melodic Interval   Harmonic Interval

DIRECTIONS: Each measure below contains an interval. Write **M** below each *melodic* interval. Write **H** below each *harmonic* interval.

sample

intervals are numbered by counting UPWARD from the bottom note to the top note. For example, the interval from A to D is a fourth (A-B-C-D). Notice that the bottom note is always counted as the first note of the interval.

signatures and accidental sharps, flats and naturals never affect the interval number. Thus all of the following examples are **4ths** because each includes **four** letters.

DIRECTION Write the correct number below each of the following harmonic intervals (8 = octave).

sample

4

DIRECTIONS: W. the correct number below each of the following melodic intervals (8 = octave).

KEYBOARD ASSIGNMENT: Play and listen to each of the intervals on this page.

Lesson 13. Intervals of the Major Scale

Name _____ Date _____ Grade _____

The staff below shows intervals using G as the lower note and notes of the G major scale as the upper notes. The *lower* note of an interval determines the KEY of the interval. The *upper* note determines the number of the interval.

An interval is called MAJOR when the upper note is in the major scale of the lower note. In the staff below, **2nds**, **3rds**, **6ths** and **7ths** are *major* intervals.

An interval is called PERFECT when the upper note is in the major scale of the lower note AND the lower note is in the major scale of the upper note. *In the staff below, **4ths**, **5ths** and **octaves** are perfect intervals. A circle has been drawn around the perfect intervals.

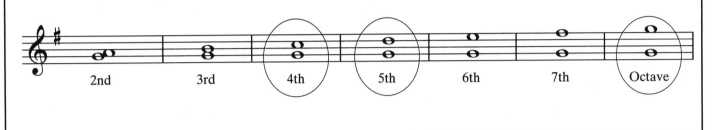

DIRECTIONS: Write the number of each interval on the line below the notes. Write the word *octave* when needed. Draw a circle around all *perfect* intervals in the staffs below. If necessary, refer to the box above.

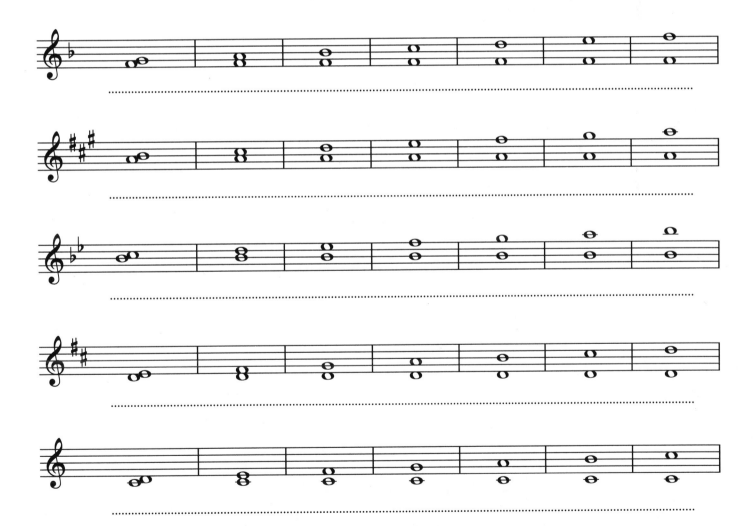

KEYBOARD ASSIGNMENT: Play and listen to each of the intervals on this page.

*Teacher's note: Explanation of the **unison** is optional. A *unison* is the interval formed when the lower note and upper note are the same. The unison is a *perfect* interval.

Lesson 14. Major and Perfect Intervals

Name_____ Date _____ Grade_____

ONLY a **2nd**, **3rd**, **6th** or **7th** can be a MAJOR interval and only when *the upper note is in the major scale of the lower note*. If a 2nd, 3rd, 6th or 7th does not meet this rule, it is *not* major, but may be a different type of interval (see Lessons 17-18-19).

ONLY a **4th**, **5th** or **octave** can be a PERFECT interval and only when *the upper note is in the major scale of the lower note AND the lower note is in the major scale of the upper note*. If a 4th, 5th or octave does not meet this rule, it is *not* perfect, but may be a different type of interval (see Lessons 18-19).

DIRECTIONS: In the following series of intervals, write the number below each interval. Use number 8 for an octave. Then write the letter M, if the interval meets the rule for *major*. Write the letter P if the interval meets the rule for *perfect*. Write a question mark (?) if the interval is neither major or perfect. Study the samples.

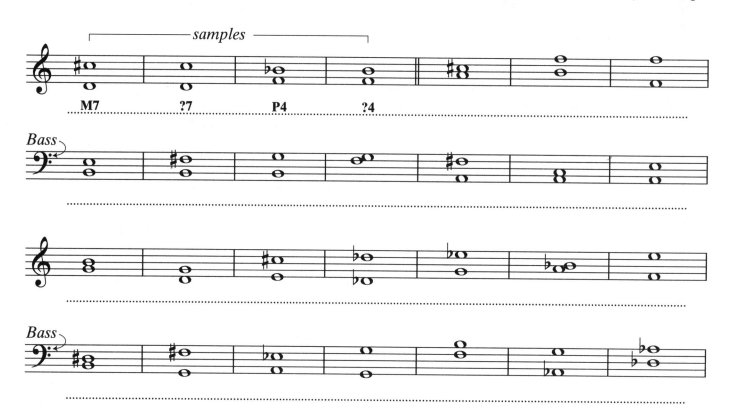

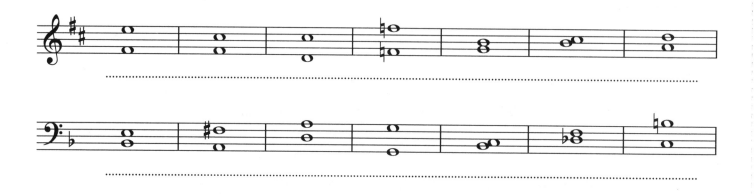

Notice the key signatures added to the next two staffs. The signatures affect the notes of the intervals, but do not change any of the rules for major or perfect intervals.

KEYBOARD ASSIGNMENT: Play and listen to each of the intervals on this page.

Lesson 15. Interval Writing

Name _____ Date _____ Grade_____

DIRECTIONS: Above each of the following notes, draw the note needed to form the interval indicated (P8 = perfect octave). If necessary, refer to the rules in Lesson 14. First, write the correct whole note, then add an accidental sharp, flat or natural, if needed. Watch for different key signatures and different clefs. Study the samples.

samples

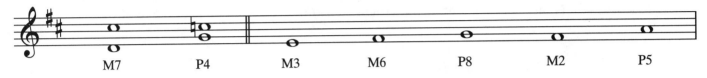

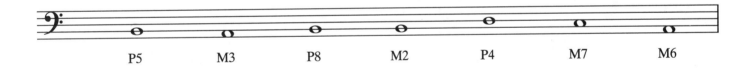

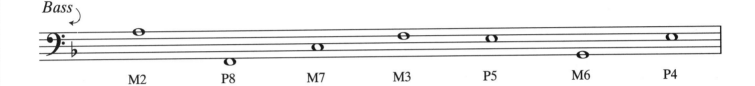

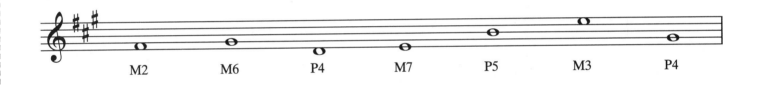

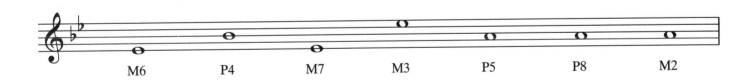

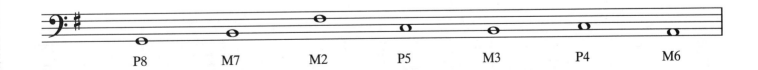

KEYBOARD ASSIGNMENT: Play and listen to each of the intervals on this page.

Lesson 16. Chromatic and Diatonic Half Steps

Name _____ Date _____ Grade_____

There are two kinds of half steps, chromatic and diatonic:

    In a **chromatic** half step, the two notes have the *same* letter name. For example, C to C♯.

    In a **diatonic** half step, the two notes have *different* letter names. For example, C to D♭.

DIRECTIONS: In the box below each of the following half steps, write **C** for *chromatic* or **D** for *diatonic*. Study the samples. Notice that some of the other half steps move up, while others move down.

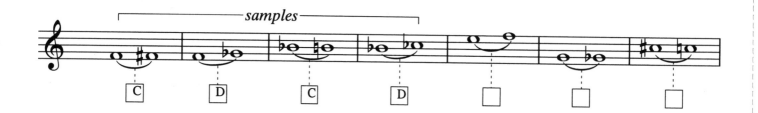

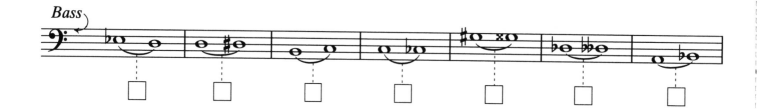

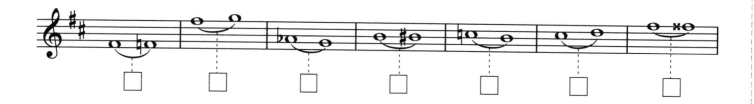

DIRECTIONS: Draw a note in each of the following measures to make the type of half step indicated. Be sure to include the correct accidental flat, sharp or natural. The half steps *may go up or down.* C = chromatic, D = diatonic.

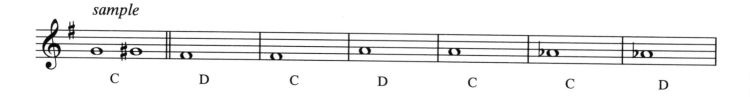

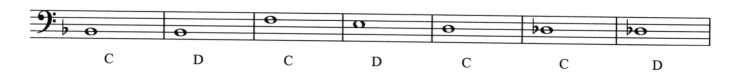

KEYBOARD ASSIGNMENT: Play and listen to all of the half steps written above.

Lesson 17. Minor Intervals

Name _____ Date _____ Grade_____

A major interval can be changed to a MINOR interval by *lowering the top note* one chromatic half step. In other words, a minor interval is a chromatic half step *smaller* than a major interval.

DIRECTIONS: Identify each of the following intervals as major or minor. Write the number name of each. Then write a *capital M* for major or a *small m* for minor. Watch for the key signature in each line. Study the samples.

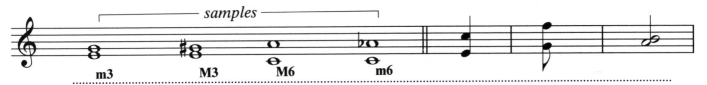

DIRECTIONS: In the following measures, draw a note *above* the printed note to make the interval indicated. Be sure to use the correct accidental flat, sharp or natural, if necessary. Watch for the key signatures.
M = major, m = minor.

KEYBOARD ASSIGNMENT: Play and listen to each of the intervals on this page.

Lesson 18. Augmented Intervals

Name _____ Date _____ Grade _____

A *major* or *perfect* interval can be changed to an AUGMENTED interval by *raising the top note* one chromatic half step. This means that an augmented interval is one chromatic half step *larger* than a major or perfect interval.

DIRECTIONS: Identify each of the following intervals as major, perfect or augmented. Write the number name of each interval. Use number 8 for an octave. Then write *capital* M (major), P (perfect) or + (augmented). Watch for the key signature in each line. Study the samples.

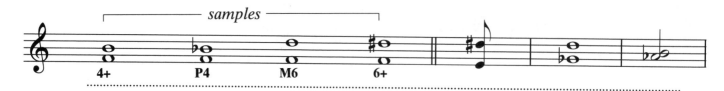

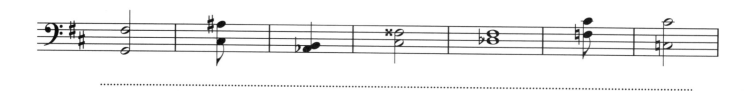

DIRECTIONS: In each measure below, draw a note above the printed note to make the interval indicated. Number 8 means an octave. Be sure to use the correct accidental flat, sharp or natural, if necessary. Watch for the key signatures.

KEYBOARD ASSIGNMENT: Play and listen to each of the intervals on this page.

Lesson 19. Diminished Intervals

Name _____ Date _____ Grade _____

A *perfect* or *minor* interval can be changed to a DIMINISHED interval by *lowering the top note* one chromatic half step. Diminished intervals are usually indicated by a degree sign. For example, 7° = diminished 7th.

DIRECTIONS: In each measure below, draw a note above the printed note to make the diminished interval indicated. Use whole notes. Watch for the key signature in each line. Study the samples.

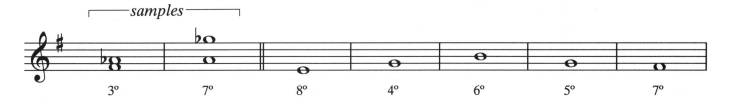

3° 7° 8° 4° 6° 5° 7°

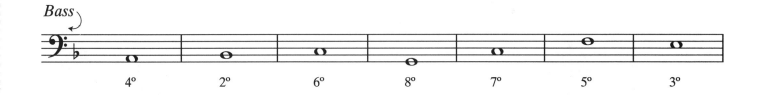

4° 2° 6° 8° 7° 5° 3°

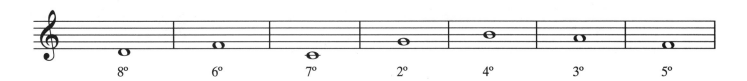

8° 6° 7° 2° 4° 3° 5°

DIRECTIONS: In each measure below, draw a note above the printed note to make the interval indicated. Number 8 means an octave. Be sure to use the correct accidental flat, sharp or natural, if necessary. Watch for the key signatures.

P5 m2 M7 3° 4+ m6 P8

6° M3 8+ 5° M2 4° m7

2° 5+ P4 8° m3 7° M6

KEYBOARD ASSIGNMENT: Play and listen to each of the intervals on this page.

Lesson 20. Inversion of Intervals

Name _____ Date _____ Grade _____

An interval may be inverted by turning it upside down. This can be done in two ways, as shown by the red arrows in these examples:

1. Move the ***upper note down*** one octave. **2.** Move the ***lower note up*** one octave.

| 2nd | 7th | 3rd | 6th | | 5th | 4th | 6th | 3rd |

DIRECTIONS: In each of the following measures, draw notes to make an inversion of the printed interval by moving the ***upper note down*** one octave. Use whole notes. Write the interval number on the line below each interval.

3   6

(sample)

DIRECTIONS: In each of the following measures, draw notes to make an inversion of the printed interval by moving the ***lower note up*** one octave. Use whole notes. Write the interval number on the line below each interval.

.4.........

(sample)

*DIRECTIONS: Write numbers to complete the following inversion chart.
        When inverted,

A 2nd becomes a _____   A 5th becomes a _____

A 3rd becomes a _____   A 6th becomes a _____

A 4th becomes a _____   A 7th becomes a _____

*Teacher's Note: You may also explain that an *octave*, when inverted, becomes a *unison* (see footnote in Lesson 13). Conversely, a *unison*, when inverted, becomes an *octave*.

Lesson 21. Interval Name Changes with Inversions

Name_____ Date _____ Grade_____

> The object of this lesson is to see how the *names* of intervals change when they are inverted. Interval names are major, minor, perfect, augmented and diminished. For example, a *major* interval becomes

DIRECTIONS: In each of the following measures, draw notes to make an inversion of the printed interval by moving the **upper note down** one octave. Use whole notes. Write the interval number and name abbreviation on the line below each interval. M = major,   m = minor,   P = perfect,   + = augmented,   ° = diminished.

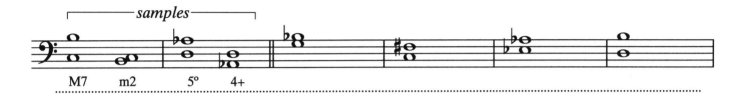

M7   m2   5°   4+

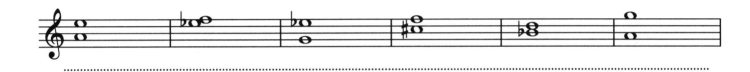

DIRECTIONS: In each of the following measures, draw notes to make an inversion of the printed interval by moving the **lower note up** one octave. Use whole notes. Write the interval number and name abbreviation on the line below each interval. M = major,   m = minor,   P = perfect,   + = augmented,   ° = diminished.

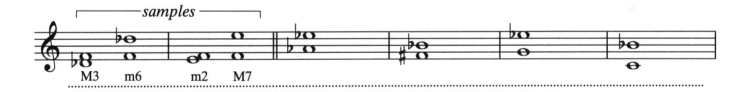

M3   m6   m2   M7

DIRECTIONS: Fill out the following inversion chart:

When inverted:

Major intervals become _____   Augmented intervals become _____

Minor intervals become _____   Diminished intervals become _____

Perfect intervals remain _____

Lesson 22. Triads

Name _____ Date _____ Grade _____

A TRIAD is a three note chord. It is written on three successive staff lines or three successive spaces of the staff. This includes leger lines and spaces.

The three notes of a triad are named (from bottom to top): ROOT, THIRD and FIFTH.

DIRECTIONS: The notes printed below are ROOTS. Draw notes a THIRD and a FIFTH above each root to form a triad. Study the sample.

DIRECTIONS: Write the letter name of the ROOT below each of the following triads. Be sure to include an accidental sharp with each letter name affected by the key signature.

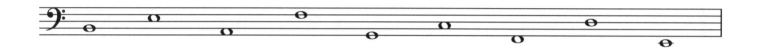

DIRECTIONS: Write the letter name of the THIRD below each of the following triads. Be sure to include an accidental flat with each letter name affected by the key signature. Notice the change of clef.

DIRECTIONS: Write the letter name of the FIFTH below each of the following triads. Be sure to include an accidental sharp with each letter name affected by the key signature. Notice the change of clef.

KEYBOARD ASSIGNMENT: Play and listen to each of the triads on this page.

Lesson 23. Triad Analysis

Name _____ Date _____ Grade _____

The interval between the ROOT and THIRD of a triad is a *major* 3rd or a *minor* 3rd.

The interval between the ROOT and FIFTH of a triad is a *perfect* 5th, *augmented* 5th or *diminished* 5th.

DIRECTIONS: Write the correct interval names of the thirds and fifths in each of the following triads. Refer to the box above. Study the samples in the first staff. Watch for changes of clef.

M = major,   m = minor,   P = perfect,   + = augmented,   ° = diminished *(see footnote)*.

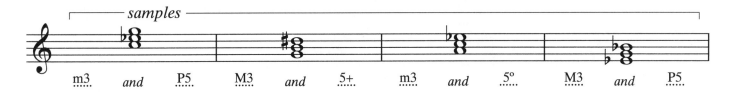

m3   *and*   P5   M3   *and*   5+   m3   *and*   5°   M3   *and*   P5

...... *and* .... *and* .... *and* .... *and* ......

...... *and* .... *and* .... *and* .... *and* ......

...... *and* .... *and* .... *and* .... *and* ......

...... *and* .... *and* .... *and* .... *and* ......

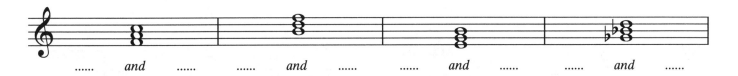

...... *and* .... *and* .... *and* .... *and* ......

These abbreviations are often used for chords: **aug** = augmented, **dim** = diminished.

KEYBOARD ASSIGNMENT: Play and listen to each of the triads on this page.

Lesson 24. More Triad Analysis

Name _____ Date _____ Grade_____

The interval between the ROOT and THIRD of a triad is a *major* 3rd or a *minor* 3rd.

The interval between the ROOT and FIFTH of a triad is a *perfect* 5th, *augmented* 5th or *diminished* 5th.

DIRECTIONS: Write the correct interval names of the thirds and fifths in each of the following triads. Refer to the box above. Study the samples in the first staff. Watch for changes of clef.

M = major,   m = minor,   P = perfect,   + = augmented,   ° = diminished.

KEYBOARD ASSIGNMENT: Play and listen to each of the triads on this page.

Lesson 25. Four Types of Triads

Name _____ Date _____ Grade_____

Triad Type:	Triad Symbol:	Consists of:	How to Form the Triad:
1. MAJOR	D	Root, M3, P5	
2. MINOR	Dm	Root, m3, P5	*Lower the 3rd of a ***major*** triad one chromatic half step.
3. DIMINISHED	D°	Root, m3, 5°	*Lower the 5th of a ***minor*** triad one chromatic half step.
4. AUGMENTED	D+	Root, M3, 5+	*Raise* the 5th of a ***major*** triad one chromatic half step.
			*See Lesson 16 for an explanation of a chromatic half step.

DIRECTIONS: Draw the necessary accidentals to make the triads indicated. In some cases a double flat (𝄫) or double sharp (𝄪) may be needed. Watch for changes of clef.

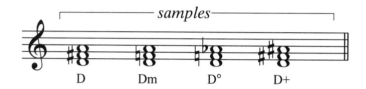

samples

D   Dm   D°   D+

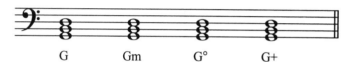

G   Gm   G°   G+

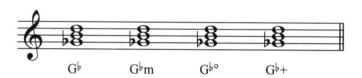

G♭   G♭m   G♭°   G♭+

F   Fm   F°   F+

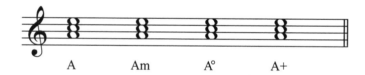

A   Am   A°   A+

E   Em   E°   E+

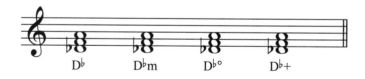

D♭   D♭m   D♭°   D♭+

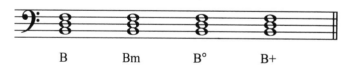

B   Bm   B°   B+

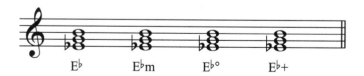

E♭   E♭m   E♭°   E♭+

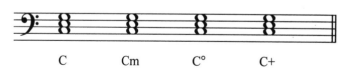

C   Cm   C°   C+

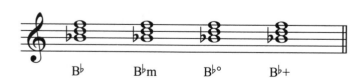

B♭   B♭m   B♭°   B♭+

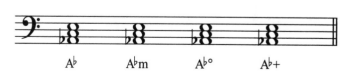

A♭   A♭m   A♭°   A♭+

KEYBOARD ASSIGNMENT: Play and listen to each of the triads on this page.

Lesson 26. Triad Identification

Name _____ Date _____ Grade _____

DIRECTIONS: Below are four types of triads. Write the letter name and triad symbol for each one. Watch for different clefs. If necessary, refer to Lesson 25.

m = minor,   + = augmented,   ° = diminished.

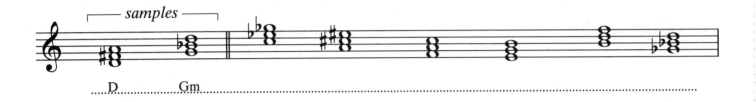

── samples ──

.......D........Gm...

Bass

....

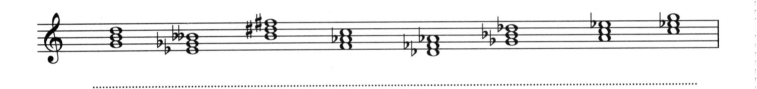

....

....

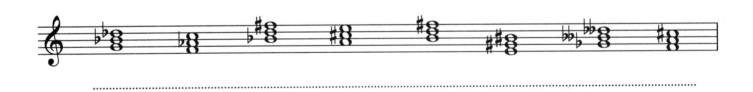

....

....

KEYBOARD ASSIGNMENT: Play and listen to each of the triads on this page.

Lesson 27. Triads of the Major Scale

Name _____ Date _____ Grade_____

Triads may be built using each note of the major scale as a root. These triads are major, minor or diminished.
Roman numerals are used to identify the ROOT and TYPE of each triad:

Major triad	(I)	Capital Roman numeral
Minor triad	(ii)	Small Roman numeral
Diminished triad	(vii°)	Small Roman numeral with degree sign

Study the samples in the staff below.

DIRECTIONS: Draw notes to form a triad above each note of the major scales below. Write Roman numerals below each triad to indicate the root and type of triad. Refer to the staff above.

DIRECTIONS: Write Roman numerals to answer the following questions:

What triads of the major scale are always *major*?   _____   _____   _____

What triads of the major scale are always *minor*?   _____   _____   _____

What triad of the major scale is always *diminished*?   _____

KEYBOARD ASSIGNMENT: Play and listen to each of the triads on this page.

Lesson 28. Major Scale Triad Analysis

Name_____ Date _____ Grade_____

Roman numerals identify two things about a triad:
> 1. The **root** of the triad.
> 2. The *type* of the triad (major, minor or diminished).

DIRECTIONS: The root of each of the following chords is a different major scale note. Beneath each triad, write the proper Roman numeral to identify the root and type of the triad. Be sure to make a clear difference between capital and small Roman numerals. Watch for different key signatures and changes of clef. If necessary, refer to the top of Lesson 27.

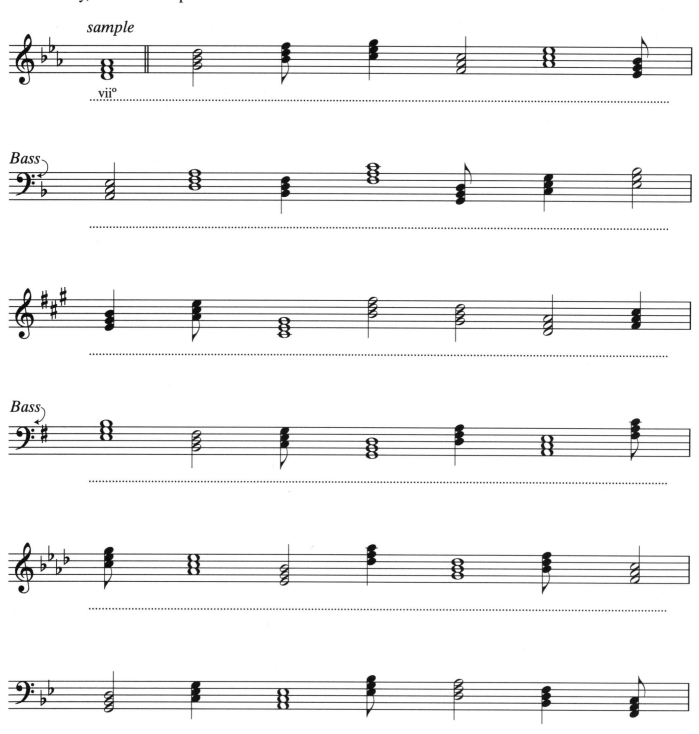

KEYBOARD ASSIGNMENT: Play and listen to each of the triads on this page.

When you have finished with this book you may go on to the Schaum HARMONY LESSONS, Book 2 (EL00374A)

Lesson 29. Schaum Harmony Quiz

Name _____ Date _____ Grade _____

DIRECTIONS: Study each of the following statements. All of the information has been presented in this book. In the answer column, write **T** (True) or **F** (False).

Answer Column

1. In flat scales the tonic is one half step above the last flat. . . . . 1._____
2. The tonic and the first scale degree are the same. . . . . 2._____
3. The upper tetrachord of D major is A B C♯ D. . . . . 3._____
4. The lower tetrachord of E major is E F G A. . . . . 4._____
5. In flat scales the upper tetrachord becomes the lower tetrachord of the next flat key. . . . . 5._____
6. The seven sharps occur in key signature order as follows: F C G D A E B. . . . . 6._____
7. The scales of C♯ and C♭ are enharmonic. . . . . 7._____
8. In key signature order, the seven flats are opposite from the seven sharps. . . . . 8._____
9. The scale of five sharps sounds exactly the same as the scale of five flats. . . . . 9._____
10. There are twelve major keys in the circle of fifths. . . . . 10._____
11. The circle of fourths moves in reverse order from the circle of fifths. . . . . 11._____
12. A melody may be transposed by using scale degree numbers. . . . . 12._____
13. Transposing a melody means writing it backwards. . . . . 13._____
14. An interval consists of three notes. . . . . 14._____
15. In a melodic interval, the notes are played together. . . . . 15._____
16. Intervals are measured from the bottom up. . . . . 16._____
17. A chromatic half step changes an interval number. . . . . 17._____
18. A diatonic half step keeps the same letter name. . . . . 18._____
19. From A up to F♯ is a major 6th. . . . . 19._____
20. From C up to F is a major 4th. . . . . 20._____
21. From E up to G is a diminished 3rd. . . . . 21._____
22. From B up to F is a perfect 5th. . . . . 22._____
23. From F♯ up to B♭ is a minor 4th. . . . . 23._____
24. From B♭ up to E is an augmented 4th. . . . . 24._____
25. The number of an interval is changed by accidentals. . . . . 25._____
26. When a major interval is inverted, it remains major. . . . . 26._____
27. When a perfect interval is inverted, it becomes minor. . . . . 27._____
28. When an augmented interval is inverted, it becomes diminished. . . . . 28._____
29. The following intervals – 2nds, 3rds, 6ths and 7ths are never perfect. . . . . 29._____
30. 4ths and 5ths cannot become minor. . . . . 30._____
31. The three notes of a triad are called 1st, 2nd and 3rd. . . . . 31._____
32. The notes A C E make a major triad. . . . . 32._____
33. The notes F♯ A C♯ make a minor triad. . . . . 33._____
34. The notes D F♯ A♯ make a diminished triad. . . . . 34._____
35. The notes B D F make an augmented triad. . . . . 35._____
36. Two types of triads are perfect and minor. . . . . 36._____
37. All major and minor triads have perfect 5ths. . . . . 37._____
38. There are seven major triads in the major scale. . . . . 38._____
39. The triad on the seventh degree of a major scale is always diminished. . . . . 39._____
40. Minor triads always occur on the 1st, 4th and 5th degrees of the major scale. . . . . 40._____

Reference Page–Major Scales with Scale Degree Numbers

C Major:

1 2 3 4 5 6 7 8

G Major:

1 2 3 4 5 6 7 8

D Major:

1 2 3 4 5 6 7 8

A Major:

1 2 3 4 5 6 7 8

E Major:

1 2 3 4 5 6 7 8

B Major:

1 2 3 4 5 6 7 8

F# Major:

1 2 3 4 5 6 7 8

F Major:

1 2 3 4 5 6 7 8

B♭ Major:

1 2 3 4 5 6 7 8

E♭ Major:

1 2 3 4 5 6 7 8

A♭ Major:

1 2 3 4 5 6 7 8

D♭ Major:

1 2 3 4 5 6 7 8

G♭ Major:

1 2 3 4 5 6 7 8

Lesson 1. Finding the Tonic

Name _____ Date _____ Grade _____

> The *first note* of a scale is called the **tonic**. It is considered the most important note of a scale. To find the tonic in sharp keys, GO UP ONE HALF STEP from the LAST SHARP (the sharp in the key signature that is farthest from the clef sign). For example, if the key signature has two sharps, the last sharp is C♯. Going up one half step from C♯ is D. Therefore, D is the tonic.

DIRECTIONS: Write the key name and draw a whole note to indicate the tonic in each of the following examples. The sample is correctly marked.

> In flat keys, the tonic has the SAME NAME as the SECOND LAST FLAT of the key signature. For example, if the key signature has three flats, the second last flat is E♭. Therefore, the tonic is E♭. Exception to the rule: if the key signature has only one flat (B♭), the tonic is F.

DIRECTIONS: Write the key name and draw a whole note to indicate the tonic in each of the following examples. The sample is correctly marked.

KEYBOARD ASSIGNMENT: Play all of the above tonic notes on the piano.

Lesson 2. Major Scale Review (Sharp Keys)

Name _____ Date _____ Grade _____

> The major scale can be divided into two tetrachords *one whole step apart*. A **tetrachord** is a series of four notes with the following intervals between them:
>
> **1** (whole step) **2** (whole step) **3** (half step) **4**
>
> The notes in each staff below form a different major scale. The first staff has the C major scale (no sharps in the key signature). The second staff has the G major scale (1 sharp in the key signature). The major scale in each staff that follows adds one more sharp to its key signature (2 sharps, 3 sharps, 4 sharps, etc.).
>
> Notice that the notes (G-A-B-C) of the **second** tetrachord of the C major scale are the *same* as the notes (G-A-B-C) of the **first** tetrachord of the G major scale on the staff below. This same tetrachord relationship continues between all of the staffs that follow. For example, the **second** tetrachord of the G major scale is the same as the **first** tetrachord of the D major scale. This is shown in the samples printed below.

DIRECTIONS: Draw whole notes for the tetrachords on the staffs below. Use the intervals: W = Whole step, H = Half step. Remember, there is also a whole step *between* the two tetrachords. Use accidental sharps as needed for the tetrachord notes; do not use key signatures. Then draw the sharps for each key signature in the column at the right.

Lesson 3. Major Scale Review (Flat Keys)

Name _____ Date _____ Grade _____

> The notes in each staff below form a different major scale. The first staff has the C major scale (no flats in the key signature). The second staff has the F major scale (1 flat in the key signature). The major scale in each staff that follows adds one more flat to its key signature (2 flats, 3 flats, 4 flats, etc.).
>
> Notice that the notes (C-D-E-F) of the **first** tetrachord of the C major scale are the same as the notes (C-D-E-F) of the **second** tetrachord of the F major scale on the staff below. This same tetrachord relationship continues between all of the staffs that follow. For example, the **first** tetrachord of the F major scale is the same as the **second** tetrachord of the B♭ major scale. This is shown in the samples printed below.

DIRECTIONS: Draw whole notes for the tetrachords on the staffs below. Use the intervals: W = Whole step, H = Half step. Remember, there is also a whole step *between* the two tetrachords. Use accidental flats as needed for the tetrachord notes; do not use key signatures. Then draw the flats for each key signature in the column at the right.

Lesson 4. Sequence of Sharp Key Signatures

Name _____ Date _____ Grade _____

> The key names of major scales with *sharps* follow part of a sequence called the **circle of 5ths** (see Lesson 8). When one sharp is added to the key signature, the scale name changes by the interval of a 5th. For example, notice that the 5th scale note of C major is G. The key signature of 1 sharp indicates the key of **G** major.
>
> key signature has no sharps: key of C major 5th scale note = G
> key signature has 1 sharp: key of G major 5th scale note = D
> key signature has 2 sharps: key of D major 5th scale note = A
>
> Samples of this sequence of 5ths are shown in the *Name of Key* column in the diagram below.
>
> The sharps in a key signature always follow the same sequence. For example, F♯ is always the first sharp, C♯ is always the second sharp, G♯ is always the third sharp, etc. This is shown in the samples printed in the diagram below.

DIRECTIONS: In the *Name of Key* column of the following diagram, write the names of all the sharp keys, following the circle of 5ths, as described above. In the remaining boxes, write the names of the sharps in each key signature.

Number of Sharps	Name of Key	1st Sharp	2nd Sharp	3rd Sharp	4th Sharp	5th Sharp	6th Sharp	7th Sharp
Zero Sharps	C							
One Sharp	G	F♯						
Two Sharps	D	F♯	C♯					
Three Sharps	A	F♯	C♯	G♯				
Four Sharps	E	F♯	C♯	G♯	D♯			
Five Sharps	B	F♯	C♯	G♯	D♯	A♯		
Six Sharps	F♯	F♯	C♯	G♯	D♯	A♯	E♯	
Seven Sharps	C♯	F♯	C♯	G♯	D♯	A♯	E♯	B♯

DIRECTIONS: Each of the following key signatures has one sharp that is wrong. Cross out the incorrect sharp in each signature. Watch for changes of clef. The sample is correctly marked.

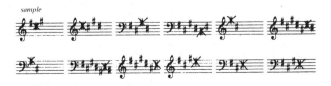

KEYBOARD ASSIGNMENT: Play the seven sharps on the piano in key signature order.

Lesson 5. Sequence of Flat Key Signatures

Name _____ Date _____ Grade _____

The key names of major scales with *flats* follow part of a sequence called the **circle of 4ths** (see Lesson 9). When one flat is added to the key signature, the scale name changes by the interval of a 4th. For example, notice that the 4th scale note of C major is F. The key signature of 1 flat indicates the key of F major.

key signature has no flats:	key of C major	4th scale note = F
key signature has 1 flat:	key of F major	4th scale note = B♭
key signature has 2 flats:	key of B♭ major	4th scale note = E♭

Samples of this sequence of 4ths are shown in the *Name of Key* column in the diagram below.

The flats in a key signature always follow the same sequence. For example, B♭ is always the first flat, E♭ is always the second flat, A♭ is always the third flat, etc. This is shown in the samples printed in the diagram below.

DIRECTIONS: In the *Name of Key* column of the following diagram, write the names of all the flat keys, following the circle of 4ths, as described above. In the remaining boxes, write the names of the flats in each key signature.

Number of Flats	Name of Key	1st Flat	2nd Flat	3rd Flat	4th Flat	5th Flat	6th Flat	7th Flat
Zero Flats	C							
One Flat	F	B♭						
Two Flats	B♭	B♭	E♭					
Three Flats	E♭	B♭	E♭	A♭				
Four Flats	A♭	B♭	E♭	A♭	D♭			
Five Flats	D♭	B♭	E♭	A♭	D♭	G♭		
Six Flats	G♭	B♭	E♭	A♭	D♭	G♭	C♭	
Seven Flats	C♭	B♭	E♭	A♭	D♭	G♭	C♭	F♭

DIRECTIONS: Each of the following key signatures has one flat that is wrong. Cross out the incorrect flat in each signature. Watch for changes of clef. The sample is correctly marked.

sample

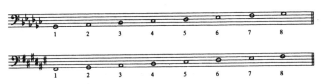

KEYBOARD ASSIGNMENT: Play the seven flats on the piano in key signature order.

Lesson 6. Comparison of Key Signatures

Name _____ Date _____ Grade _____

DIRECTIONS: Fill in the boxes below, listing the order of sharps and flats as indicated. The starting box is filled in as a sample. Fill in the remaining boxes.

SHARPS IN KEY SIGNATURE ORDER						
1st	2nd	3rd	4th	5th	6th	7th
F♯	C♯	G♯	D♯	A♯	E♯	B♯

FLATS IN KEY SIGNATURE ORDER						
1st	2nd	3rd	4th	5th	6th	7th
B♭	E♭	A♭	D♭	G♭	C♭	F♭

Now write them in reverse order. Notice that flats are put first.

FLATS IN REVERSE ORDER						
7th	6th	5th	4th	3rd	2nd	1st
F♭	C♭	G♭	D♭	A♭	E♭	B♭

SHARPS IN REVERSE ORDER						
7th	6th	5th	4th	3rd	2nd	1st
B♯	E♯	A♯	D♯	G♯	C♯	F♯

Notice the following patterns in the sequence of key signature letter names:
Flats in *reverse* order = Sharps in *regular* order.
Sharps in *reverse* order = Flats in *regular* order.
This will help you to remember the order of sharps and flats in key signatures.

THE SCALES OF C, C♯ AND C♭

DIRECTIONS: On the staffs below, write the notes for the scales of C, C♯ and C♭. Notice that the notes of the C scales are either *all* natural, *all* sharp or *all* flat.

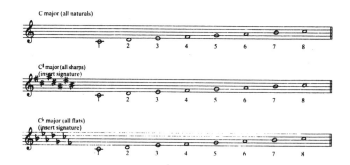

KEYBOARD ASSIGNMENT: Play the major scales of C, C♯ and C♭.

Lesson 7. Enharmonic Keys

Name _____ Date _____ Grade _____

Enharmonic keys sound the same, but are *spelled differently*. For example, the key of D♭ major sounds the same as the key of C♯ major. D♭ major is easier to read because there are 5 flats in the key signature, whereas C♯ major has 7 sharps in the key signature.

DIRECTIONS: On the staffs below, draw the notes of the two enharmonic scales, D♭ major and C♯ major.

G♭ major and F♯ major are also *enharmonic*. One key signature has 6 flats, the other has 6 sharps. However, G♭ major is used more often in music literature.

DIRECTIONS: On the staffs below, draw the notes of the two enharmonic scales, G♭ major and F♯ major. Watch for the clef sign.

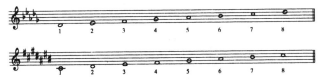

B major and C♭ major are also *enharmonic*. B major is easier to read because there are 5 sharps in the key signature, whereas C♭ major has 7 flats in the key signature.

DIRECTIONS: On the staffs below, draw the notes of the two enharmonic scales, B major and C♭ major. Watch for the clef sign.

KEYBOARD ASSIGNMENT: Play each pair of enharmonic scales on the piano. Notice that they sound exactly alike.

Lesson 8. Major Key Circle of Fifths

Name _____ Date _____ Grade _____

DIRECTIONS: In each section of the large circular staff, draw the notes of the first **five** scale degrees, going upward. Notice that the **5th** degree of each scale is always the 1st degree of the scale that follows it. Draw the new key signature each time, and write the 1st and 5th letter names in the boxes below the staff.

Compare your answers with the key letter names in the small circle in the center of the diagram. If your answers are correct, they will match with the clockwise letter sequence of the inner circle.

The scales of B major, G♭ major and D♭ major are to be used instead of their *enharmonic* equivalents (C♭ major, F♯ major and C♯ major).

Notice when you finish that you have returned to the same note on which you started.

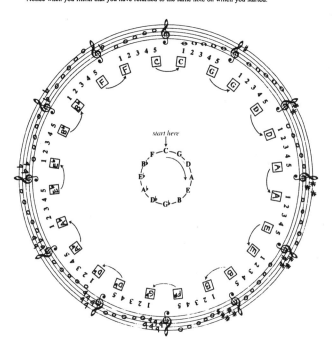

KEYBOARD ASSIGNMENT: Play the major key circle of fifths on the piano, going up five steps each time, just as written.

Lesson 9. Major Key Circle of Fourths

Name_____ Date_____ Grade_____

DIRECTIONS: In each section of the large circular staff, draw the notes of the first **four** scale degrees, going upward. Notice that the **4th** degree of each scale is always the 1st degree of the scale that follows it. Draw the new key signature each time, and write the 1st and 4th letter names in the boxes below the staff.

Compare your answers with the key letter names in the small circle in the center of the diagram. If your answers are correct, they will match with the clockwise letter sequence of the inner circle.

The scales of D♭ major, G♭ major and B major are to be used instead of their enharmonic equivalents (C♯ major, F♯ major and C♭ major).

Notice when you finish that you have returned to the same note on which you started.

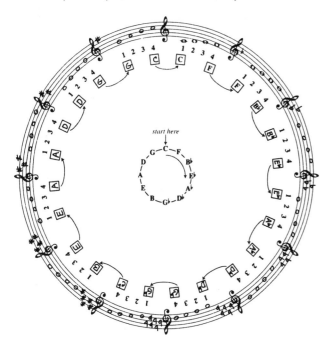

KEYBOARD ASSIGNMENT: Play the major key circle of fourths on the piano, going up four steps each time, just as written. Notice that order of keys in the circle of fourths is the *reverse* of the order in the circle of fifths.

Lesson 10. Scale Number Names

Name_____ Date_____ Grade_____

> The notes of a major scale are numbered 1 through 8. These numbers are sometimes called **degrees**. The 1st scale degree is the same as the *tonic* note (see Lesson 1).

DIRECTIONS: On the staffs below, draw the appropriate scale note above each number. Watch for **changes of clef**.

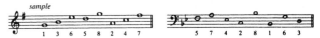

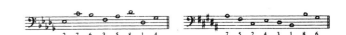

KEYBOARD ASSIGNMENT: Play all the scale notes you have written above.

Lesson 11. Transposing with Scale Degree Numbers

Name_____ Date_____ Grade_____

> An excerpt from "Blue Bells of Scotland" is printed here, with scale degree numbers below each note. The measures at the end of each staff have notes and scale degree numbers from other keys. These are to be used as reference when doing the transposing on this page.

DIRECTIONS: Transpose the melody "Blue Bells of Scotland," to the five keys indicated below. Refer to the scale degree numbers at the end of each staff. Watch for different key signatures.

KEYBOARD ASSIGNMENT: Play the excerpt from "Blue Bells of Scotland" in each of the transposed keys.

Lesson 12. Melodic and Harmonic Intervals

Name_____ Date_____ Grade_____

> An **interval** is the distance between two notes. Two notes, played *one after the other*, are a **melodic** interval. Two notes played *together* are a **harmonic** interval. This is shown in the following examples:

Melodic Interval   Harmonic Interval

DIRECTIONS: Each measure below contains an interval. Write **M** below each *melodic* interval. Write **H** below each *harmonic* interval.

> Intervals are numbered by counting UPWARD from the bottom note to the top note. For example, the interval from A to D is a fourth (A-B-C-D). Notice that the bottom note is always counted as the first note of the interval.
> Key signatures and accidental sharps, flats and naturals never affect the interval number. Thus all of the following examples are **4ths** because each includes **four** letters.

DIRECTIONS: Write the correct number below each of the following harmonic intervals (8 = octave).

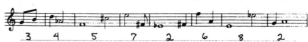

DIRECTIONS: Write the correct number below each of the following melodic intervals (8 = octave).

KEYBOARD ASSIGNMENT: Play and listen to each of the intervals on this page.

Lesson 13. Intervals of the Major Scale

Name _____ Date _____ Grade _____

The staff below shows intervals using G as the lower note and notes of the G major scale as the upper notes. The *lower* note of an interval determines the KEY of the interval. The *upper* note determines the number of the interval.

An interval is called MAJOR when the upper note is in the major scale of the lower note. In the staff below, **2nds**, **3rds**, **6ths** and **7ths** are *major* intervals.

An interval is called PERFECT when the upper note is in the major scale of the lower note AND the lower note is in the major scale of the upper note. *In the staff below, **4ths**, **5ths** and **octaves** are perfect intervals. A circle has been drawn around the perfect intervals.

DIRECTIONS: Write the number of each interval on the line below the notes. Write the word *octave* when needed. Draw a circle around all *perfect* intervals in the staffs below. If necessary, refer to the box above.

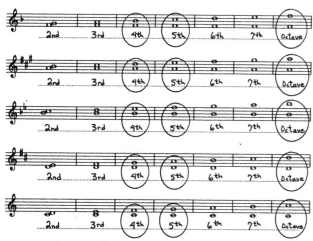

KEYBOARD ASSIGNMENT: Play and listen to each of the intervals on this page.

*Teacher's note: Explanation of the **unison** is optional. A *unison* is the interval formed when the lower note and upper note are the same. The unison is a *perfect* interval.

Lesson 14. Major and Perfect Intervals

Name _____ Date _____ Grade _____

ONLY a **2nd**, **3rd**, **6th** or **7th** can be a MAJOR interval and only when *the upper note is in the major scale of the lower note*. If a 2nd, 3rd, 6th or 7th does not meet this rule, it is *not* major, but may be a different type of interval (see Lessons 17-18-19).

ONLY a **4th**, **5th** or **octave** can be a PERFECT interval and only when *the upper note is in the major scale of the lower note AND the lower note is in the major scale of the upper note*. If a 4th, 5th or octave does not meet this rule, it is *not* perfect, but may be a different type of interval (see Lessons 18-19).

DIRECTIONS: In the following series of intervals, write the number below each interval. Use number 8 for an octave. Then write the letter M, if the interval meets the rule for major. Write the letter P if the interval meets the rule for perfect. Write a question mark (?) if the interval is neither major or perfect. Study the samples.

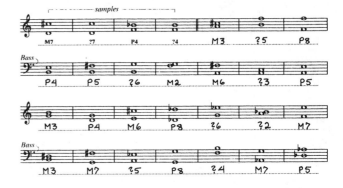

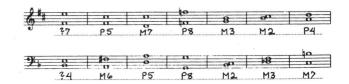

Notice the key signatures added to the next two staffs. The signatures affect the notes of the intervals, but do not change any of the rules for major or perfect intervals.

KEYBOARD ASSIGNMENT: Play and listen to each of the intervals on this page.

Lesson 15. Interval Writing

Name _____ Date _____ Grade _____

DIRECTIONS: Above each of the following notes, draw the note needed to form the interval indicated (P8 = perfect octave). If necessary, refer to the rules in Lesson 14. First, write the correct whole note, then add an accidental sharp, flat or natural, if needed. Watch for different key signatures and different clefs. Study the samples.

KEYBOARD ASSIGNMENT: Play and listen to each of the intervals on this page.

Lesson 16. Chromatic and Diatonic Half Steps

Name _____ Date _____ Grade _____

There are two kinds of half steps, chromatic and diatonic:

In a **chromatic** half step, the two notes have the *same* letter name. For example, C to C♯.

In a **diatonic** half step, the two notes have *different* letter names. For example, C to D♭.

DIRECTIONS: In the box below each of the following half steps, write **C** for *chromatic* or **D** for *diatonic*. Study the samples. Notice that some of the other half steps move up, while others move down.

DIRECTIONS: Draw a note in each of the following measures to make the type of half step indicated. Be sure to include the correct accidental flat, sharp or natural. The half steps *may go up or down*. C = chromatic, D = diatonic.

KEYBOARD ASSIGNMENT: Play and listen to all of the half steps written above.

Lesson 17. Minor Intervals

A major interval can be changed to a MINOR interval by *lowering the top note* one chromatic half step. In other words, a minor interval is a chromatic half step *smaller* than a major interval.

DIRECTIONS: Identify each of the following intervals as major or minor. Write the number name of each. Then write a *capital M* for major or a *small m* for minor. Watch for the key signature in each line. Study the samples.

DIRECTIONS: In the following measures, draw a note *above* the printed note to make the interval indicated. Be sure to use the correct accidental flat, sharp or natural, if necessary. Watch for the key signatures. M = major, m = minor.

KEYBOARD ASSIGNMENT: Play and listen to each of the intervals on this page.

Lesson 18. Augmented Intervals

A *major* or *perfect* interval can be changed to an AUGMENTED interval by *raising the top note* one chromatic half step. This means that an augmented interval is one chromatic half step *larger* than a major or perfect interval.

DIRECTIONS: Identify each of the following intervals as major, perfect or augmented. Write the number name of each interval. Use number 8 for an octave. Then write *capital M* (major), P (perfect) or + (augmented). Watch for the key signature in each line. Study the samples.

DIRECTIONS: In each measure below, draw a note above the printed note to make the interval indicated. Number 8 means an octave. Be sure to use the correct accidental flat, sharp or natural, if necessary. Watch for the key signatures.

KEYBOARD ASSIGNMENT: Play and listen to each of the intervals on this page.

Lesson 19. Diminished Intervals

A *perfect* or *minor* interval can be changed to a DIMINISHED interval by *lowering the top note* one chromatic half step. Diminished intervals are usually indicated by a degree sign. For example, 7° = diminished 7th.

DIRECTIONS: In each measure below, draw a note above the printed note to make the diminished interval indicated. Use whole notes. Watch for the key signature in each line. Study the samples.

DIRECTIONS: In each measure below, draw a note above the printed note to make the interval indicated. Number 8 means an octave. Be sure to use the correct accidental flat, sharp or natural, if necessary. Watch for the key signatures.

KEYBOARD ASSIGNMENT: Play and listen to each of the intervals on this page.

Lesson 20. Inversion of Intervals

An interval may be inverted by turning it upside down. This can be done in two ways, as shown by the red arrows in these examples:

1. Move the *upper note down* one octave.   **2.** Move the *lower note up* one octave.

DIRECTIONS: In each of the following measures, draw notes to make an inversion of the printed interval by moving the *upper note down* one octave. Use whole notes. Write the interval number on the line below each interval.

DIRECTIONS: In each of the following measures, draw notes to make an inversion of the printed interval by moving the *lower note up* one octave. Use whole notes. Write the interval number on the line below each interval.

*DIRECTIONS: Write numbers to complete the following inversion chart.
When inverted,

A 2nd becomes a 7th   A 5th becomes a 4th
A 3rd becomes a 6th   A 6th becomes a 3rd
A 4th becomes a 5th   A 7th becomes a 2nd

*Teacher's Note: You may also explain that an *octave*, when inverted, becomes a *unison* (see footnote in Lesson 13). Conversely, a *unison*, when inverted, becomes an *octave*.

Lesson 21. Interval Name Changes with Inversions

Name _____ Date _____ Grade _____

The object of this lesson is to see how the *names* of intervals change when they are inverted. Interval names are major, minor, perfect, augmented and diminished. For example, a *major* interval becomes

DIRECTIONS: In each of the following measures, draw notes to make an inversion of the printed interval by moving the **upper note down** one octave. Use whole notes. Write the interval number and name abbreviation on the line below each interval. M = major, m = minor, P = perfect, + = augmented, ° = diminished.

DIRECTIONS: In each of the following measures, draw notes to make an inversion of the printed interval by moving the **lower note up** one octave. Use whole notes. Write the interval number and name abbreviation on the line below each interval. M = major, m = minor, P = perfect, + = augmented, ° = diminished.

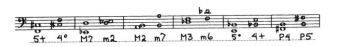

DIRECTIONS: Fill out the following inversion chart:

When inverted:

Major intervals become _minor_ Augmented intervals become _diminished_

Minor intervals become _major_ Diminished intervals become _augmented_

Perfect intervals remain _perfect_

Lesson 22. Triads

Name _____ Date _____ Grade _____

A TRIAD is a three note chord. It is written on three successive staff lines or three successive spaces of the staff. This includes leger lines and spaces.

The three notes of a triad are named (from bottom to top): ROOT, THIRD and FIFTH.

DIRECTIONS: The notes printed below are ROOTS. Draw notes a THIRD and a FIFTH above each root to form a triad. Study the sample.

DIRECTIONS: Write the letter name of the ROOT below each of the following triads. Be sure to include an accidental sharp with each letter name affected by the key signature.

DIRECTIONS: Write the letter name of the THIRD below each of the following triads. Be sure to include an accidental flat with each letter name affected by the key signature. Notice the change of clef.

DIRECTIONS: Write the letter name of the FIFTH below each of the following triads. Be sure to include an accidental sharp with each letter name affected by the key signature. Notice the change of clef.

KEYBOARD ASSIGNMENT: Play and listen to each of the triads on this page.

Lesson 23. Triad Analysis

Name _____ Date _____ Grade _____

The interval between the ROOT and THIRD of a triad is a *major* 3rd or a *minor* 3rd.

The interval between the ROOT and FIFTH of a triad is a *perfect* 5th, *augmented* 5th or *diminished* 5th.

DIRECTIONS: Write the correct interval names of the thirds and fifths in each of the following triads. Refer to the box above. Study the samples in the first staff. Watch for changes of clef.
M = major, m = minor, P = perfect, + = augmented, ° = diminished (see footnote).

These abbreviations are often used for chords: **aug** = augmented, **dim** = diminished.

KEYBOARD ASSIGNMENT: Play and listen to each of the triads on this page.

Lesson 24. More Triad Analysis

Name _____ Date _____ Grade _____

The interval between the ROOT and THIRD of a triad is a *major* 3rd or a *minor* 3rd.

The interval between the ROOT and FIFTH of a triad is a *perfect* 5th, *augmented* 5th or *diminished* 5th.

DIRECTIONS: Write the correct interval names of the thirds and fifths in each of the following triads. Refer to the box above. Study the samples in the first staff. Watch for changes of clef.
M = major, m = minor, P = perfect, + = augmented, ° = diminished.

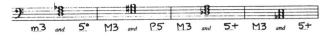

KEYBOARD ASSIGNMENT: Play and listen to each of the triads on this page.

Lesson 25. Four Types of Triads

Name _____ Date _____ Grade_____

Triad Type:	Triad Symbol:	Consists of:	How to Form the Triad:
1. MAJOR	D	Root, M3, P5	
2. MINOR	Dm	Root, m3, P5	*Lower the 3rd of a *major* triad one chromatic half step.
3. DIMINISHED	D°	Root, m3, 5°	*Lower the 5th of a *minor* triad one chromatic half step.
4. AUGMENTED	D+	Root, M3, 5+	*Raise the 5th of a *major* triad one chromatic half step.
			*See Lesson 16 for an explanation of a chromatic half step.

DIRECTIONS: Draw the necessary accidentals to make the triads indicated. In some cases a double flat (♭♭) or double sharp (×) may be needed. Watch for changes of clef.

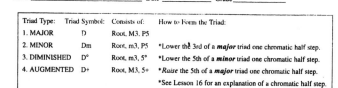

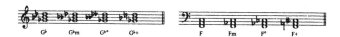

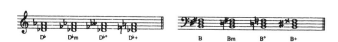

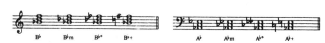

KEYBOARD ASSIGNMENT: Play and listen to each of the triads on this page.

Lesson 26. Triad Identification

Name _____ Date _____ Grade_____

DIRECTIONS: Below are four types of triads. Write the letter name and triad symbol for each one. Watch for different clefs. If necessary, refer to Lesson 25.

m = minor,   + = augmented,   ° = diminished.

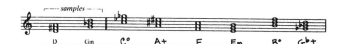

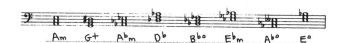

KEYBOARD ASSIGNMENT: Play and listen to each of the triads on this page.

Lesson 27. Triads of the Major Scale

Name _____ Date _____ Grade_____

Triads may be built using each note of the major scale as a root. These triads are major, minor or diminished. Roman numerals are used to identify the ROOT and TYPE of each triad:

Major triad (I) Capital Roman numeral
Minor triad (ii) Small Roman numeral
Diminished triad (vii°) Small Roman numeral with degree sign

Study the samples in the staff below.

DIRECTIONS: Draw notes to form a triad above each note of the major scales below. Write Roman numerals below each triad to indicate the root and type of triad. Refer to the staff above.

DIRECTIONS: Write Roman numerals to answer the following questions:

What triads of the major scale are always *major*?   I   IV   V

What triads of the major scale are always *minor*?   ii   iii   vi

What triad of the major scale is always *diminished*?   vii°

KEYBOARD ASSIGNMENT: Play and listen to each of the triads on this page.

Lesson 28. Major Scale Triad Analysis

Name _____ Date _____ Grade_____

Roman numerals identify two things about a triad:
1. The *root* of the triad.
2. The *type* of the triad (major, minor or diminished).

DIRECTIONS: The root of each of the following chords is a different major scale note. Beneath each triad, write the proper Roman numeral to identify the root and type of the triad. Be sure to make a clear difference between capital and small Roman numerals. Watch for different key signatures and changes of clef. If necessary, refer to the top of Lesson 27.

KEYBOARD ASSIGNMENT: Play and listen to each of the triads on this page.

When you have finished with this book you may go on to the Schaum HARMONY LESSONS, Book 2 (EL00374A)

Lesson 29. Schaum Harmony Quiz

Name _____ Date _____ Grade _____

DIRECTIONS: Study each of the following statements. All of the information has been presented in this book. In the answer column, write **T** (True) or **F** (False).

Answer Column

1. In flat scales the tonic is one half step above the last flat.	1.	F
2. The tonic and the first scale degree are the same.	2.	T
3. The upper tetrachord of D major is A B C♯ D.	3.	T
4. The lower tetrachord of E major is E F G A.	4.	F
5. In flat scales the upper tetrachord becomes the lower tetrachord of the next flat key.	5.	F
6. The seven sharps occur in key signature order as follows: F C G D A E B.	6.	T
7. The scales of C♯ and C♭ are enharmonic.	7.	F
8. In key signature order, the seven flats are opposite from the seven sharps.	8.	T
9. The scale of five sharps sounds exactly the same as the scale of five flats.	9.	F
10. There are twelve major keys in the circle of fifths.	10.	T
11. The circle of fourths moves in reverse order from the circle of fifths.	11.	T
12. A melody may be transposed by using scale degree numbers.	12.	T
13. Transposing a melody means writing it backwards.	13.	F
14. An interval consists of three notes.	14.	F
15. In a melodic interval, the notes are played together.	15.	F
16. Intervals are measured from the bottom up.	16.	T
17. A chromatic half step changes an interval number.	17.	F
18. A diatonic half step keeps the same letter name.	18.	F
19. From A up to F♯ is a major 6th.	19.	T
20. From C up to F is a major 4th.	20.	F
21. From E up to G is a diminished 3rd.	21.	F
22. From B up to F is a perfect 5th.	22.	F
23. From F♯ up to B♭ is a minor 4th.	23.	F
24. From B♭ up to E is an augmented 4th.	24.	T
25. The number of an interval is changed by accidentals.	25.	F
26. When a major interval is inverted, it remains major.	26.	F
27. When a perfect interval is inverted, it becomes minor.	27.	F
28. When an augmented interval is inverted, it becomes diminished.	28.	T
29. The following intervals – 2nds, 3rds, 6ths and 7ths are never perfect.	29.	T
30. 4ths and 5ths cannot become minor.	30.	T
31. The three notes of a triad are called 1st, 2nd and 3rd.	31.	F
32. The notes A C E make a major triad.	32.	F
33. The notes F♯ A C♯ make a minor triad.	33.	T
34. The notes D F♯ A♯ make a diminished triad.	34.	F
35. The notes B D F make an augmented triad.	35.	F
36. Two types of triads are perfect and minor.	36.	F
37. All major and minor triads have perfect 5ths.	37.	T
38. There are seven major triads in the major scale.	38.	F
39. The triad on the seventh degree of a major scale is always diminished.	39.	T
40. Minor triads always occur on the 1st, 4th and 5th degrees of the major scale.	40.	F